FIRST HISTORY

THE NORMANS

Anne and Barry Steel

Illustrated by Gerry Wood

ROURKE ENTERPRISES, INC.
Vero Beach, Florida 32964

First published in the
United States in 1987 by
Rourke Enterprises, Inc.
PO Box 3328, Vero Beach,
Florida 32964

First published in 1986 by Wayland (Publishers) Ltd
61 Western Road, Hove, East Sussex BN3 1JD, England

© Copyright 1986 Wayland (Publishers) Ltd

Phototypeset by Kalligraphics Ltd, Redhill, Surrey
Printed in Italy by G. Canale & C.S.p.A., Turin

All the words which appear in **bold**
are explained in the glossary
on page 24.

Library of Congress Cataloging-in-Publication Data
Steel, Anne.
    The Normans.
    (First history)
    Bibliography: p.
    Includes index.
    Summary: Explains who the Normans were, how they
took over England in 1066, and life in those times.
    1. Great Britain — History — History period, 1066–1154 —
Juvenile literature.   2. Normans — England — Social life
and customs — Juvenile literature.   3. England — Social
life and customs — Medieval period, 1066–1485 —
Juvenile literature.   [1. Great Britain — History —
Norman period, 1066–1154.   2. Normans — England —
Social life and customs.   3. England — Social life
and customs — Medieval period, 1066–1485]   I. Steel,
Barry.   II. Wood, Gerald, ill.   III. Title.   IV. Series.
DA195.S74   1987   942.02   86–20231
ISBN 0–86592–162–8

Contents

Who were the Normans?

In about A.D. 850 fierce Vikings from
northern Europe attacked France. The
French King gave some land to their
chief, Rollo, to make them leave France
in peace. This land was called
Northmannia, land of the Northmen.
Later the name changed to Normandy

More Vikings came to live in Normandy. They became **Christians**, married French people, and learned to speak French. They became known as Normans. They were brave fighters and wanted to conquer new lands. The picture opposite shows some Norman soldiers ready for battle.

The most famous Norman was William the Conqueror.

William the Conqueror

A **Saxon** lord named Harold promised to help William become King of England. When Harold was made king himself, William was very angry. He sailed to England with a large army, in ships like the ones in the picture below.

William's army fought a battle against
Harold near Hastings in A.D. 1066. The
fighting was very fierce, as you can see
from this picture. Harold was killed, and
William became King of England.

William was very cruel to people who did
not do as he wanted. He soon ruled every
part of England.

Village life

Most Normans lived in country villages called **manors**. Each manor belonged to a rich lord. Poor people, like the ones in the picture below, were allowed to grow crops

on the lord's land. Around the village was the **common land**. Villagers used this to graze animals and collect berries, nuts and wood. The family in the picture below are giving part of their crops to their lord. Everyone had to do this.

William the Conqueror sent men to every part of England to make a list of all the buildings and land in each manor. This list was called the Domesday Book.

Town life

Norman towns were quite small. Most of them grew up around markets like the one in the picture below. Most of the people made or sold things at the market. London was the largest town. It had markets, fairs and fine stores. All towns had walls to protect them.

Towns were dirty places. People threw garbage into the street and there were animals everywhere. Few towns had clean water, and many people became ill. The buildings were made of wood and built close together, so fires started easily and spread quickly.

At home

Poor people lived in huts of one room with mud walls and **thatched** roofs. They slept on the floor with their animals. Some wealthier people might have a **loft**. Rich people had stone houses, often with two floors. But even they would have animals

like pigs and chickens in their house. The Normans ate simple food like rye bread, fruit, peas, beans and fish. Meat was often eaten by rich people like those in this picture, but it was a special treat for the poor. After a meal, leftovers were thrown on the floor for the animals.

Sports and entertainment

Fighting was a favorite Norman sport. Knights on horseback tried to knock each other to the ground. You can see them fighting with lances and shields in the picture opposite. Rich Normans loved hunting and **hawking**. Many Normans enjoyed music and dancing. **Minstrels,**

jugglers and acrobats traveled around from place to place. Short plays of Bible stories were acted in churches and market places. The Normans played a kind of soccer with many players on each side. Richer people played indoor games like checkers and chess.

15

The law and the people

In Norman times there was a lot of crime.
There were no policemen. Each lord had
to catch criminals in his own village.
Sometimes he tried them in his own **court**,
and sometimes they were sent to the
the county court for **trial**.

The Normans had cruel punishments.
Sometimes hands or feet were cut off.
People were hanged for crimes like
murder, stealing and **poaching** deer from
the King's forests. No wonder the
poachers in the picture opposite look
frightened! The men in the picture above
are fighting to settle a quarrel. This was
called trial by battle.

Castles

The Normans built castles to help them keep order in their new kingdom. The first ones were wooden, like the **motte and bailey** castle below. But they soon started building stone castles. These had a **moat** around them and a high wall or fence. Inside were many different buildings. The

strongest and most important building
was the keep, where the lord, his family
and men lived. This picture shows the
inside of a Norman keep. It must have
been cold, dark and gloomy. At the center
of the castle was the great hall where
meals were eaten.

Churches and monasteries

The Normans built beautiful churches, cathedrals and abbeys. They took many years to finish. Norman buildings often had round arches, as you can see in this picture of Durham Cathedral.

Many people became **monks** or **nuns** and
went to live in monasteries or convents.
They had to get up long before dawn,
work very hard, and spend many hours
praying. Monasteries and convents
provided beds for weary travelers, and
free food for the poor. They cared for the
sick and ran schools. In the picture below,
an **archbishop** is visiting a monastery.

Things to do

Castle

Look carefully at pictures of Norman castles. Make walls from cardboard and use cardboard tubes for round towers. Make a hill out of chicken wire covered with papier-mâché.

Knight's shield

Cut a shield shape (see picture on page 7) from stiff cardboard or posterboard. Glue narrow strips of cardboard around the edges for extra strength. Draw a design on your shield and paint it.

Glossary

Archbishop   The most important priest in England.
Christians   People who believe in Jesus Christ.
Common land   Land that everyone in a village could use.
Court   A place where people are brought for **trial**.
Hawking   A sport in which trained hawks are set free to hunt other birds and animals.
Loft   A space right underneath the roof of a building.
Manors   The name given to Norman villages and the land around them.
Minstrels   People who made a living by singing or playing a musical instrument.
Moat   A ditch dug around a castle and filled with water.
Monks   Men who went to serve God in a monastery.
Motte and bailey   An early kind of castle.
Nuns   Women who went to serve God in a convent.
Poaching   Stealing animals, fish or birds from someone's land.
Saxons   People who lived in England before the Normans came.
Thatched roofs   Roofs made from straw or reeds.
Trial   A way of proving whether or not someone has done something wrong.

Index